CANADA

☆ National Capital
● Province/Territory Capital

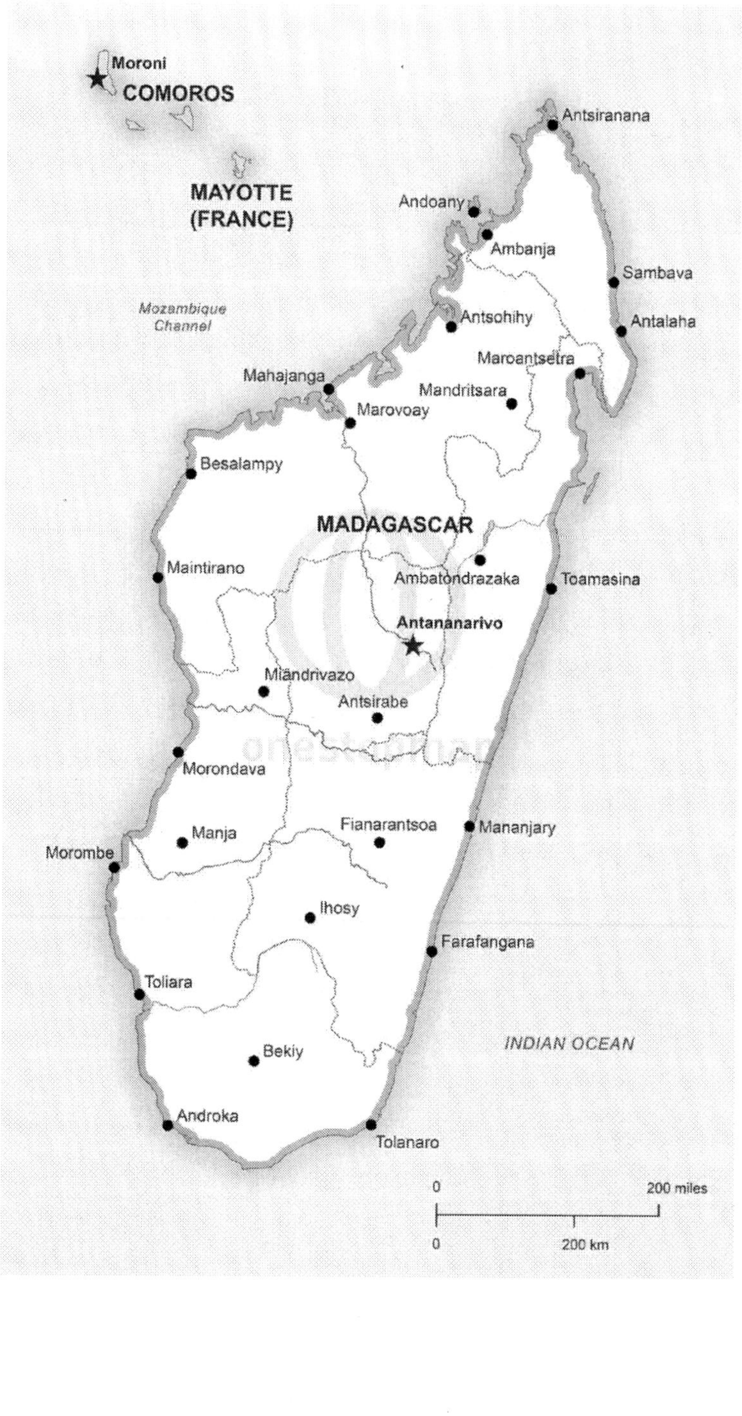

Moroni
COMOROS
MAYOTTE
(FRANCE)
Mozambique
Channel
Antsiranana
Andoany
Ambanja
Sambava
Antsohihy
Antalaha
Maroantsetra
Mahajanga
Mandritsara
Marovoay
Besalampy
MADAGASCAR
Maintirano
Ambatondrazaka
Toamasina
Antananarivo
Miandrivazo
Antsirabe
Morondava
Manja
Fianarantsoa
Mananjary
Morombe
Ihosy
Farafangana
Toliara
INDIAN OCEAN
Bekiy
Androka
Tolanaro
0
200 miles
0
200 km

Stories from my youth in Canada and Madagascar

Leif G. Stolee

Mimast Inc

* * * * *

This paperback edition published in 2019 by Mimast Inc

Copyright © Mimast Inc 2019,

Canadian ISBN 978-1-987926-18-7

All rights reserved.
No part of this publication may be reproduced, stored in a retrieval system, or transmitted in any form or by any means, electronic, mechanical, photocopying, recording or otherwise, without the prior written permission of the Publishers.

The rights of Leif G Stolee to be identified as the author of this Work have been asserted by him in accordance with the Copyright, Designs and Patents Act 1988.

* * * * *

All enquiries regarding this paperback edition to

Mimast Inc
Arnhem Road
Duncan
British Columbia V9L 3A7
Canada

Acknowledgements

I am grateful to the many people who have encouraged me to publish these true stories and who have helped in the production of this book by editing my text and by providing illustrations and photographs.

I should like especially to thank my wife, Liz, and my publisher, Michael, for their patience, understanding and support.

Needless to say, any mistakes, in grammar and spelling, and errors in facts are my fault entirely. Nobody else is to blame.

Author's Note

My Norwegian grandparents emigrated to settle eventually in Canada. My mother, Ragna Lefsrud, was one of eight siblings. My first story is about her youngest brother.

My father, Peter Stolee, served three terms as a Lutheran missionary in Madagascar where I, with my sister and two brothers, spent most of my formative years and had most of the following adventures.

James   Erling   Leif
Peter (father)   Elinor (sister)   Ragna (mother)

The Stories

Tony The Christmas Turkey 9

The Bloody Flux 11

Earliest Memories: Learning to Walk 13

Father Drives the Water from the Milk 15

Feeding the Bull 19

Assigned to Lea Park 21

The Worst Day of My Life 25

Little Gravestones 29

Great Map 31

Sharks 35

The Great Garden 39

Catching Moray Eels 43

Crocodiles 47

Removing a Tribal Curse 51

Messing around in Boats 55

About the author 57

MIM

Tony The Christmas Turkey

My grandparents, John and Karen Lefsrud, had a large family starting with Gullick, Alf, Sigurd, Helga, Ragna, and Ivor who were born in Kalispell, Montana. After moving to Canada, when free land was being offered to homesteaders in 1905, the family lived in Westaskwin for little over a year, where a baby was born who died soon after birth. Restless as ever, John decided to move on and the family travelled to Northern Alberta when they established a homestead near Gruoard, where Sybille and Tony were born.

Tony was born after the death of the baby boy who had died in Wetaskwin so, understandably, he was an object of great concern to his mother. She became so ill after his birth that John gave Tony to an Indian woman to wet nurse until Karen was better. The Indian lady took good care of him. She fed him regularly and put him into a papoose lined with moss to take care of his bodily functions,

Tony flourished 'like a green bay tree" as the poet has it, and it was only after considerable time that Karen was able to take him back from his wet nurse and care for him herself. Naturally Tony became her favourite. She fed him and cuddled him to the degree that he became a little 'butter ball' darling of his doting mother! Tony learned to love his food, a habit that stayed with him and his waist all his life.

His older siblings, amused by their rolly polly little brother, decided to have a bit of fun with him. Sometime in November they told him that he was getting all those goodies and special treats because his mother was fattening him up to be the Christmas turkey. Poor Tony was alarmed but because he couldn't resist all good things, he just kept on eating. However, as the preparations for a good old fashioned Norwegian Christmas began in December his brothers kept whispering their dire warnings and Tony was not able to dismiss his growing anxiety. Soon, even eating did not have a calming effect.

In mid December, surrounded by the sights and sounds of his impending doom, Tony began to really worry. Of course, frequent reminders of how delicious he would be as a substitute turkey only added spurs to the fears that rode him.

So Tony began to look for a solution and being a bright little boy, decided that if he were too skinny to make a good 'turkey' that he would not end up on the Christmas table. So, as far as possible Tony started to slow down his eating.

His mother, knowing how much Tony enjoyed his food, simply could not understand why he was off his feed. Finally, one morning, Tony simply stopped eating. This, of course, brought the matter to a head, and after close and persistent questioning, Tony finally told his mother that he was determined not to be the Christmas Turkey.

Karen, outraged, told John what the older boys had done, demanding that they be severely disciplined for terrifying their little bother in such a cruel fashion. John, however, bursting into howls of laughter, was so disarmed that he was unable to do anything at all except give them a scolding.

Thus the story of Tony the Christmas Turkey became a Christmas classic among the Lesfruds just as Charles Dickens' 'Christmas Carol' has become a classic to the rest of the world.

*****

The Bloody Flux

I was only six months old in 1929 when my Norwegian parents returned to Canada from their sabbatical as Lutheran missionaries so I had no memory at all of Madagascar. Having heard my parents talk so often about the island, it was firmly fixed in my mind that the sooner we got back there the better. We eventually returned to Madagascar in 1936.

It is ironic therefore that one of my earliest memories of Madagascar is of lying exhausted in a bed and being pinned down by my Father, to prevent my squirming, while a man in a white coat pushed a long needle attached to a large syringe into my stomach, slowly filling me with lots of warm water. To my horror this living nightmare was repeated several times. That was my first introduction to one of the most deadly diseases in Madagascar - enteric dysentery.

In early times since the European exploration of the tropics, *The Bloody Flux,* was the cause of countless deaths among sailors, traders and others. Its most famous victim, Sir Francis Drake, died of it in 1596, after his unsuccessful attack on the Spanish in the Caribbean at San Juan, Puerto Rica.

In the case of enteric dysentery, bacteria attack the hair-like villi lining of the intestine which absorbs nutrients, causing internal bleeding, with death resulting from dehydration and loss of blood. Since pure sea water has many of the qualities of blood and is readily absorbed, in those early days it was injected into the intestines to prevent dehydration which, even though the bleeding may have stopped, the dehydration eventually causes death. It obviously was a 'Hail Mary Solution!' Fortunately in my case it worked!

In developed countries, dysentery causes stomach pains and frequent passing of stool. Medical relief being readily available, severe discomfort lasts for two to three days and normally disappears within a week. But to us, in Madagascar in 1937, the 'bloody flux' was a matter of life or death.

After my attack, I was very weak and it took a long time before I was even able to get out of bed. Much later on, when talking about my memories of the doctor and the great needle, Father told me that when I finally did recover, the calves of my legs were not thicker than his two fingers. I must have looked like someone on the point of death from starvation.

Luckily, I never got dysentery again, only periodic bouts of malaria, worms, blood poisoning from an infected cut, and other children's diseases such as chicken pox, mumps, and frequently infected toes from parash (a tick that lays eggs between the toes and under the toe nails, eggs that gradually develop into a large itchy white sac filled with many squirming offspring.)

In 1942, before being transferred from Ranomafana (in Fianarantsoa) to Fort Dauphin (in Tolanaro), to run the Twelve Man School, (where catechists were trained to assist the native pastors and missionaries from all the Lutheran mission stations across Southern Madagascar), my Father also came down with dysentery. Fortunately we were staying at our summer cottage at Lebanon, just outside Fort Dauphin at that time, it being the hot season, Dr. Faget, the French colonial medical officer was readily available.

Despite the usual medications and procedures Father's condition worsened rapidly so the doctor decided to inject him with sea water. I remember Erling and me running down to West Beach, Erling wading into the calmer water just inside the curve of the reef, swirling the pail in the sea to make certain it was clean, and filling it half full of crystal clear sea water. I remember standing outside the bedroom while Dr. Faget plunged a large syringe into Father filling his intestines full of sea water. And I remember the anxious days of waiting to see if he would get better.

Father was very lucky, as sea water injections were really an act of desperation on the part of the doctor. Many others were not so fortunate. I recalled that Reverend Carlson had died from dysentery at Lebanon about five of six years earlier.

* * * * *

Earliest Memories: Learning to Walk

My earliest memory is of an old man holding me up by my hands, placing my feet on his feet and walking me around three large rooms, the sitting room, dining room, and study of the large Lefsrud farm house which he had built about twelve miles directly north of Viking, Alberta. Around and around, day after day I was patiently 'walked,' for the odd reason that I did not know how to walk. I had skipped the crawling to walking stage and developed a swift sliding along on my bottom propelled by the energetic use of my arms.

The reason for this failure to go through the normal stage of crawling to walking was that just when I was beginning to change over from crawling to walking, my father and mother were making the long voyage from Madagascar to Alberta, Canada by ship. The first leg of the journey, from Madagascar to Marseille via the Suez Canal took considerable time and the plan to prevent the possibility of me tottering along the deck and falling overboard was to empty one of the large drawers in their cabin and keep me there in safety (outside the necessary time for feeding, changing etc.)

On the second lap of the journey, from Le Havre to New York or Montreal (I don't know which) on a much larger transatlantic liner on a much rougher ocean, they took the same precautions. The end result was that although my grandparents were delighted to see me, they were shocked at the fact that of all their grand children I was the only one who showed no desire to walk. Thus my grandfather's determination that he would teach me to walk.

Death

Another faint memory I have, of the time when we were staying at the Lefsrud homestead, was of looking at a large polished wooden box placed on chairs in the centre of the living room and people walking quietly around the box and being very sad because there was a man in the box. It was the coffin of my Uncle Ivor, a medical doctor who had hit his head and had been killed when he fell off a motor driven speeder which jumped the rails west of Edson.

Living in St Paul

I have slightly clearer memories of when we lived in St. Paul where the family was located when father attended a Lutheran Seminary in order to become an ordained pastor. I remember running across the grass through the water spraying out of a garden hose on a hot day and how much we enjoyed it.

I also remember Christmas Eve when I was given a little red wheelbarrow that my father had made for me. Also, I remember sitting on the upper stair, looking down on a strange man singing Christmas carols in a loud voice. (It being the height of the depression, apparently mother and dad had invited an unemployed stranger to spend Christmas Eve with them.)

I have a third very vivid memory of the tall china cabinet in the dining room being suddenly halted in its tumble, after it tipped in its attempt to squash me flat. My father leapt up just in time to save me and those few dishes that had not already crashed on the floor.

The reason for this escapade and ensuing narrow escape is that in those days it was fashionable to have little stands on which knives and forks rested beside the dinner plate. My mother had bought little stands that were elongated lions, the knives and forks resting between the lion's head the tail. While the rest of the family and their guests were eating Sunday dinner, I had left the table and crawled over to the china cabinet, opened the swinging door and started to climb up the shelves to reach the lions. In doing so, I tipped the china cabinet. Luckily only a few of mother's best dishes paid the price of my impulsive folly.

*****

Father Drives the Water from the Milk

There may be an improvement in the milk-producing capacity of Malagasy cows these days since, when Father and Mother were in Madagascar, native cattle were not noted for their bountiful milk. Some time in the distant past the hump-backed Zebu or Omby, as the natives called them, arrived from Africa and were highly valued as the most important measure of a person's wealth and status. They were bred for size and strength as they were used to trample the terraced rice fields which were flooded each spring so the individual rice shoots could be planted in the softened mud. They were also vital for sacrificial purposes at weddings and funerals, for ensuring good fortune and for appeasing offended spirits.

Unfortunately, the Zebu were very poor dairy cattle; a Holstein or Guernsey would have been considered a miracle to milk production, almost the bovine counterpart of the goose that laid the golden egg. So, missionary families needing milk, had to get the word out to the surrounding villages. The natives would collect the milk in small wooden bowls with a spout and pour the milk into empty wine bottles. They would then attach three or four bottles at either end of a bamboo pole and walk with it, from anywhere up to ten kilometres to the mission station.

No Vazaha* ever drank the milk that was not carefully boiled to kill off the multitude of germs which lined the wooden bowls or the bottles which, though rinsed, were never sterilised. Of course since the amount of milk produced by a single cow was not that great, milkmen, firm believers in the *caveat emptor,*** found it hard to resist the temptation of augmenting their profit by adding water to the milk. As a result, the resident cook would test each bottle of milk with an hydrometer to see if water had been added and if it exceeded a small amount of watering, for reasonable profit, the bottle would be rejected.

The milk purchased would immediately be boiled to kill off any germs; this was 'home-grown pasteurisation.' It was very difficult to judge just how long the milk should be kept at the boil and, since it was much better to be safe than sorry, the milk that we drank almost always had a sort of 'burnt' taste. That is why (except for the time when Madagascar was under the control of the Vichy government and was being blockaded) our breakfast bowls of rice were all given a large spoonful of Nestle's condensed milk.

Well it happened that Father's assignment during his first term was to run the Lutheran Mission High School for Malagasy boys at Manantantely in Toliara. To be able to do so, he not only had to have a B. Ed (University of Alberta) but he also had to spend nearly a year in Paris attending the Alliance Francais to be certified as a principal of an accredited high school in a French colony.

Thus it was that one of the educational props used to teach human anatomy was a plaster of Paris model of a human body, standing about five feet high, divided down the centre with one side having normal white skin from the crown of the head to the feet. The other side of the mannequin showed what a man would look like if he were skinned alive, muscles around a glaring eye, ear, jaws, neck, shoulders, chest, stomach, bowels, abdomen, buttocks, thighs, knees, legs and feet.

In addition, all the inner organs of the body such as the brain, heart, lungs, liver, intestines, kidneys, bowels, etc. were individualised in bright colours and could be unhooked from the body cavity. Thus students were not only able to see the human body, skin and exterior muscles and but could learn where the organs were located and could also open them to examine their inner parts.

One day Father was moving the mannequin from one building to another on the school grounds. Covered with a white cloth and standing on a little platform carried by two students, it happened to pass the residence and, of course, the detached kitchen where the milkmen were sitting around passing the time of the day while waiting for the cook to evaluate and pay for their milk.

Ever curious those milkmen asked, "Rangay!*** What do you have under that white cloth?"

"Friends," Father replied, "I have no desire to cause you needless fear. It is really something that you really don't want to know about, let alone look at. It would not be proper for me to alarm you."

"Rangay!" they begged, "We're not children. We are not men to be easily alarmed. Surely it must be something of great interest."

"Well, if you insist!" Father said. Whipping off the covering sheet, he revealed the half-skinned mannequin to the terrified milkmen. There was a collective gasp of horror and then a scream. "Who is that?" they yelled.

"That," Father replied, "is the last man who put water into the milk."

Shouting in terror, they leaped to their feet, grabbed their bottles and scattered in all directions. The next morning there wasn't a milkman in sight.

Needless to say, it took weeks of explanations and negotiations to get the milkmen to resume deliveries. I don't think that Mother was at all impressed.

---

* Vazaha - foreigner - the common name applied to anyone from overseas such as Whites, Arabs, Indians, Chinese, etc.

** caveat emptor   - Latin: buyer beware. A guiding principle of many business men

*** Rangay - a term of respect, a combination of *Elder, Sir, Teacher, Leader, Boss, etc.*

* * * * *

Feeding the Bull

The Lefsrud house and barn were much more imposing than the Stolee's homestead. The house was a large two story building, including a full basement and also a large attic where we used to go and play with our uncles' and aunts' childhood toys.

The barn was a magnificent red building having about ten large stalls running down each side. It had a great big hay loft with a Dutch gabled roofing with a peaked front to which a pulley was attached so that large bales of hay, oats, etc. could be hauled up for storage. Above each stall there was a square hole cut in the loft flooring so that the animals could easily be fed by pushing the hay down into their mangers.

Being by nature very curious, I used to follow my uncles around when they did the chores. I was fascinated by how the animals were fed. I was especially drawn to the bull, a great Hereford with great horns and a large brass ring in its nose.

One peaceful Sunday afternoon I snuck out of the house when the rest of the family was taking life easy and wandered over to the barn to look at the animals. The thought struck me that maybe the bull, a great red Hereford with a white face, whom I admired so greatly, would like to have an afternoon snack. So I climbed with some difficulty up the ladder to the loft, grabbed a hay fork and piled up a goodly amount of hay beside the bull's feeding hole.

I then started to push the hay down to the bull who, lowering his great head into the manger, gave thanks to the Lord, and started eating enthusiastically. Peering down I saw that I was not feeding him fast enough, so I made a large pile of hay over the hole and tried to push it down with the fork. Instead of going down the hay jammed the hole. Well that was a problem easily solved. I started to push the hay down with my foot. Suddenly a great batch of hay went down hole with me on top of it.

Fortunately the bull, hearing the noise, lifted his head to look up when I came tumbling past his nose into the manger. The bull, grateful for the additional hay, lowered his head and kept on eating. Looking up at his great white face, large mouth and ring in his nose, I took the only action possible. I burrowed to the bottom of the manger under the hay. I lay as quietly as possible watching the bull slowly working his way through his large lunch. I was terrified that when he got to me he would finish me off for dessert.

I lay there as quietly as a mouse for well over an hour while the bull, taking the required twenty chews per mouthful as his mother had taught him, quietly munched his way through the hay. Once my beating heart had slowed down to a reasonable pace, I began to wonder if there was any way out that would not startle the bull. Eventually, I noticed that the manger was constructed with two by two by fours across the front to keep the hay from falling on the stall floor. Along each side, the boarding stopped about a foot above the flooring. So I very quietly crawled under the boarding to the next stall, fortunately empty, climbed out of the manger, ran out of the barn and promptly started to bawl as loudly as possible.

Out of the house came my mother and the others overjoyed at finding me. They had been searching for me all over the house and yard for well over an hour. The hugs and kisses were most welcome; being told I could not go into the barn on my own was not welcome.

* * * * *

Assigned to Lea Park

By the time Father had completed his theology degree and was a duly ordained pastor, the great depression of the Nineteen Thirties had so severely curtailed the finances of the Norwegian Lutheran Church that it was unable to send its normal complement of missionaries back to Madagascar. As a result, Father accepted a call to Lea Park, a dirt poor rural congregation north of Vermillion, near the Saskatchewan border.

The parsonage in Heinsburg, being the only home of the widow of the former pastor, Father scouted around and came across an old abandoned log cabin of a trapper who hopefully had gone to a far better place. It was built on a hillside not far from the country church about a half mile away.

The cabin was about twelve feet wide and eighteen feet long at most. The usual insulation between the logs was cracked and dried. The bottom log rested on the wooden floor which had been laid over logs which were dug into the bare ground. To prevent the inflow of frigid air, it had been a custom to pile manure against the bottom log and the flooring just before freeze up. Unfortunately that precaution had not been taken before we moved in.

It had an old ineffective wood burning stove, two single paned windows on each side, a single door on the right hand wall and a draughty old outdoor toilet that was sheer torture to use when temperatures dropped below zero. There being no well, the water had to be hauled up daily from a farm across the road and down the hill.

My Father had been born in 1895 and raised in a sod house in the Dakota Territories. As eldest son, he had played a vital role in the family homesteading in Alberta in 1905. Only an instinctive pioneer would have dared move his wife and four children into such primitive conditions. Now, Ragna, my mother, had come from a well-established farming family near Viking and had always lived in reasonable comfort. My father must have had great persuasive powers to get her to agree to move into such a dilapidated hovel.

Two double bunks were fixed up at the end of the cabin, James and I sleeping in the lower bunk and Erling on top. Elinor slept in the lower bunk across from us; her upper bunk was used for storage. A large steamer trunk was parked on the floor between the bunks. A curtain was hung between the bunk bedroom, leaving the rest of the cabin for the kitchen shelves, cupboards, kitchen table, four chairs and a rocking chair. That same space also housed Mother and Father's bed, a book shelf, the stand for the water pail, the wood box, additional suitcases, cloth hangers on the wall, and the rest of our worldly goods.

Since we did not have coal, it was impossible to bank the fire so it would last all night. By morning it often got so cold that the water pail would be frozen solid. The cabin was lined with heavy brown packing paper and at night the heads of the nails holding the paper in place would be coated with frost caused by our breathing. When Father was away, Mr. Lear, the farmer who brought us the water every morning, would light the stove if Mother had not done so earlier.

To add to our discomfort, the cabin was infested with bed-bugs and every morning we would tally the number we had killed from the smears of blood on the 'wall paper.' We had a little evening poem that went:

> Good Night. Sleep tight.
> Don't let the bedbugs bite.
> If they do, take a shoe
> And beat them till they're black and blue!

The blood bath ended when we finally had the cabin fumigated. By the spring of 1935, Father, thinking it might be long time before we would return to Madagascar, built a properly insulated single room addition on the front that was double the size of the original cabin. It had a new kitchen, cupboards, an effective proper wood burning range, double paned windows, screens, book shelves, and additional furniture. The original log cabin became the bedrooms. Although the vertical siding was not painted, we were convinced that we lived in a mansion. Ironically we had barely settled into our comfortable surroundings when Father was asked to return to Madagascar. It was a welcome invitation to a far more comfortable way of life.

I don't have many clear memories of Lea Park but a few stand out in my mind. One is of trudging to the top of the hill with our sleighs and sliding down to the cabin. Another was wading in the little stream during the spring run-off. I fell madly in love with Lena the farmer's daughter at the bottom of the hill. I also recall the funeral in the little church. A local bachelor and handy man had died suddenly. After the service there were many comments about how he loved a cup of coffee when visiting his neighbours so I concluded that he died from too much coffee.

My most vivid memory, however, is of the Christmas program of 1934. It was held in the country schoolhouse that was about three quarters of a mile from our cabin. It was a very cold night and we traveled in a little wooden cab with a small glass window in front, equipped with heater and lamp. It had room enough for eight or ten people. The whole outfit, mounted on a farmer's working wagon, was drawn by a team of puffing, steaming horses, guided by reins through a small slit below the cab window. I don't remember anything of the program except Elinor standing on the darkened stage reciting Longfellow's "I heard the bells on Christmas day, their old familiar carols play", while being accompanied by someone playing that haunting tune on the piano.

It made a vivid impression on me, especially the lines *"For hate is strong and mocks the song of Peace on Earth, Good will to men."* Her recital gave me a distinct shove on my life-long love of poetry. It may have also laid the grounds that transformed her into such a wonderful poet. Despite all our differences, Elinor knew how much I loved the wonderful poems she sent me over the years.

*****

The Worst Day of My Life

Since my parents returned to Canada in December, 1929, when I was less than six months old, I have no memories at all of Madagascar before Father's second term. Under normal circumstances they would have returned to the mission field after father had completed two years at the Lutheran Seminary in St. Paul to become a pastor. However, in his first term, my father had also gone to Madagascar with a Bachelor of Education degree from the University of Alberta and a certification by the Sorbonne in Paris as qualified to teach in a French colony. He had determined to take this step because often, when he got into a discussion or argument with his fellow missionaries, they would say or imply something along these lines: "Stolee you really aren't qualified to make a judgement. You are only a teacher, not a preacher."

When he became ordained, the Great Depression of the Nineteen Thirties was at its height and the Norwegian Lutheran Church of America simply did not have sufficient funds to maintain its contingent of missionaries at full strength, neither in Madagascar nor China. So, Father accepted a call as a fully-fledged minister to the a poverty-stricken Lutheran congregation at Lea Park, Alberta.

Thus my first sketchy memories are of the Lefsrud farm (my grandparent's) near Viking, the house in Como Park where we lived when Father went to seminary and the Stolee farm near Donalda. It was only after we settled into the little, old, two room trapper's cabin in Lea Park, that my memory was jolted into a some sort of sequential coherence by the ravenous bedbugs that infested the primitive parsonage.

Naturally Mother and Father would often talk about Madagascar, hoping that it would soon be financially feasible for the Church to send them back. So, it became natural for us children to think of Madagascar as our real "home land" - a wonderful place "over the rainbow" where our family really belonged.

When the Church's finances finally improved, we left Lea Park for France in late December, 1935 and arrived in Fort Dauphin in early February, 1936. Naturally Elinor, Erling, little James and I thought we had arrived at the promised land. I, at least, hadn't a clue that our stay was to be very brief at the pleasant vacation cottage at Lebanon, where the cool ocean breezes swept the small peninsula two miles south of Fort Dauphin.

Even though Father had left for the mission station in Ranomafana (Hot Water) some weeks earlier, the idea that my mother was about to abandon us was simply inconceivable. When we were moved into the Missionary Children's Boarding School in Fort Dauphin (otherwise know as the McChicken House) and Mother and James went back to Lebanon, I began to realise that something had gone seriously wrong.

Even so, I was astonished when Mother turned up, in a sedan chair, and James, in a small, peaked roofed, latticed cage lined with bedding and pillows. The chair was carried by four husky men. The cage, which was very light and attached to a bamboo rod, was carried by two other men. The next thing I knew I was being hugged and kissed, told to be a good boy, obey Miss Thompson, always tell the truth and say my prayers. I was stunned when Mother got back into her sedan chair which was hoisted onto the shoulders of the carriers who promptly took off on the road to Mount Bezavona (Big Fog). James followed in his little cage. Suddenly the full horror struck me!

I took off running as fast as I could after them, expecting of course that Mother would stop, pick me up and take me with her. Nothing doing! The carriers broke into a rapid trot knowing that they would have to get to the foot of the coastal mountain range, about thirty miles to the north east, before night fall. The next day they would start out early to climb the narrow trail over Tsi Tonga Barika (Barrels can't come) Mountain and down into the Ambolo valley to Ranomafana, about ten miles from the pass.

I burst out into tears and just kept on running. Mother stopped for a moment, explaining that they had to go to Ranomafana and pleading with me to stop following her, she begged me to go back to the Home. Not on my life! I just kept crying and running as fast as I could on my short little legs. By the time I had reached the outskirts of the town I was exhausted! I simply quit! I watched them slowly shrink in size and then disappear around a curve in the road. I just sat down and bawled my eyes out.

There was nothing more to do. I turned and walked, crying all the way back to the Home. There, a few older children having already gone through the sorrow of separation, laughed and called me a cry baby.

Miss Thompson, however, having witnessed such scenes so often, did her best to comfort me. May she rest in peace!

Of course I recovered. After all, the disappearance of a mother is not the end of the world, even to a child. I am convinced, however, that being abandoned by my mother has had a long term traumatic effect on me. I developed a strong stammer and stutter that has never really left me. There remains a deep wound on my soul that, like a stigmata, periodically oozes anxiety. I have never been able to shake the underlying sense of insecurity that haunts me even *"when peace like a river attendeth my way,"* as the old hymn has it.

* * * * *

Climbing mountains is thirsty work for young Leif Stolee

Little Gravestones

The mountains bordering the Ambolo Valley were formed originally from layers of igneous rock and which had been folded by tectonic forces over millions of years. Although they were heavily forested, there were areas of rock made bare by the folding process and constant exposure to the hot sun. This resulted in large slabs being separated from the rock below; longitudinal cracks ran the length of the exposures. The Tanosy tribal people made their gravestones from these surface layers of igneous rock.

Having found a suitable surface layer, they would lay down a long narrow pile of wood about sixteen to thirty six inches from the edge of the overlap. The pile extended anywhere from eight to sixteen feet along the crack. They would set the wood on fire and keep it going until the slab reached the desired heat. Then they would brush away the embers and douse the heated area with buckets of cold water. The rock would snap along the heated line. Voila! They would have gravestones that ranged from six feet to sixteen feet in length and a foot and a half to three feet wide. One end would be dug into the ground and the larger part would stand erect in their grave yards.

The greater the wealth or status of the deceased, the greater the gravestone. The greater the gravestone, the greater the slaughter of their horned cattle. The more horns mounted beside the gravestone, the greater the period of mourning. The greater the eating and drinking (usually rum), the louder the mourning, wailing and drumming. At the death of a chief, the funeral rites might well go on for over a week.

The Stolee family outside their cottage in Madagascar.

Elinor   Ragna(mother)   Peter (father)
                   James   Erling   Leif

* * * * *

Great Map

During one Short Vacation, Father told us that according to Tanosy folklore, the Ambolo valley had been inhabited by Vazimba (Little People)* long before they themselves had arrived by outrigger canoes from the Indonesian archipelago around the first millennium BC. As evidence, he had heard that there were grave stones of the Vazimba on the shoulder of one of the mountains to the east separating the valley from the sea.

Ever curious, Erling and I, armed with a lunch, set out one morning to walk about six miles across the valley, climb to the shoulder and find that there were, indeed, gravestones just below the peak; they were between three and five feet high. It was very moving to be looking out over the valley and imagining the Little People being driven back up the mountain with now only a few small gravestones to mark their last stand.

Erling   **Leif**

It was a memorable day and at supper we told everyone about our great adventure. Father was particularly interested to know if we liked climbing the mountain, how often we had to rest and if we found our trip very tiring. No problem! Us tired? It was a cake walk! We could have gone twice as far and scaled far higher peaks without even breaking out into a sweat!

We didn't know that Father, who really had much more than his share of "natural smarts" had learned a great deal about surveying from being raised in a pioneering family and from being trained as a fighter pilot during the First World War. We also didn't know he had an ulterior motive for his questioning - a wall sized map of the Ambolo Valley that would accurately pinpoint the many small villages scattered across his small "mission field." We also didn't realise that, while he had the "brains," he had no intention of wasting his time doing the leg work necessary to make an accurate map.

So, we were rather surprised a few mornings later when Father came out of his study carrying a collapsible tripod, a small carpenter's level, a large board about twenty inches square (with a hole in the centre) covered with paper, a long narrow home-made ruler with a door latch attached to one end. At one end, there was a moveable piece with a narrow slot set at a right angle to the ruler. There was also a thin nail set at a right angle at the other. There was a larger removable nail, to fix the ruler to the centre of the board, and a large magnetic compass.

He took us outside, mounted the board on the tripod, levelled it, centred the ruler by pushing the nail into the hole in the middle of the board, sighted the mountain peak to the east of us, drew a line on the along the side of the ruler, placed the compass on the line and wrote the magnetic bearing of the peak (something around 090 degrees or so.) He then told us that this was going to be the base line between the Station and the Little People's Peak.

He had Erling who was twelve years old and two years my senior taking a few practice runs until he was very adept at taking bearings, replacing the paper, re-taking careful bearings himself on the fresh paper and labelling them. He then pointed at Tsi Tonga Barika to the south, a mountain to the north, two additional peaks on the east side of the valley and one on the west side on the valley. Next he told Erling to record all their bearings not only from Little People's Peak, but also from each additional peak as we climbed them.

So, rather than wasting Father's valuable time by running the ferry or playing beside the river, Erling and I climbed each peak, took the required bearings and got a clean paper for each climb. To help us on our way, he gave us a few sandwiches and a couple of canteens of water. Father would thank us after each climb, probably further rewarding us with a couple of francs each, so we could buy candy from the local Chinese store. He then set to work on the sheets of data he had accumulated.

All he had to do to get an accurate scale of distance was to measure out a base line of one hundred metres along the top of our hill, take a bearing from each end of Little People's Peak and by triangulation establish its distance in kilometres from our hill. Then, by transferring the bearings from the sheets that Erling had brought back and applying the length of a kilometre from his original base line, Father had his large scale map of his "mission field" in the Ambolo Valley.

* The Vazimba, according to popular belief, were the first inhabitants of Madagascar. They are generally described as a pygmy people, probably as distinct and ancient as the Australian aborigines, who migrated from the islands of modern-day Indonesia around 350 BC. According to folklore they were eventually annihilated by the arrival of normal-sized Malagasy people who came, centuries later from the same Pacific islands. Stories about the Vazimba form a significant element in the cultural history and collective identity of the Malagasy people, ranging from the historical to the supernatural, inspiring diverse beliefs and practices across the island.

* * * * *

MİM

Sharks

Fort Dauphin's inner harbour was nestled just below the Fort and the Colonial Administrative buildings on the headland. It was provided a small degree of protection in the long curving bay stretching north towards Mount Bezavona (Big Fog), and east past Vinany Kely (Little Lagoon) and then on to Evitraha. A light house marked the eastern end of the peninsula about twelve miles north of Fort Dauphin. The small cove was protected by a long pier on cement piles, which allowed the currents to clear the harbour's basin. The pier was linked to a massive curved cement two-stepped breakwater, its high outer wall protecting the much larger storage and loading area.

It was from here that rawhides of the Zebu, the humped Malagasy cattle, great boxes of split mica, castor beans, sisal, industrial garnets, etc. were loaded by stevedores or by cranes into the barges which were either rowed or towed by a tug to the ships anchored in the less protected waters of Fort Dauphin's open bay. Such produce was shipped primarily to Europe. In turn, goods unloaded at the pier were sent to various destinations all across Southern Madagascar.

Normally the inner harbour, well protected by the pier and curving breakwater, was a safe place to swim and was used regularly by the French. Their pre-school children often played in the shallow waters along the shore under the watchful eyes of their Malagasy nannies. One Saturday Philip, Paul, Charles and I were hanging around the pier watching the barges being loaded when suddenly I noticed a shark slowly swimming where some children were playing in the water. Yelling a warning, we dashed down from the pier into the water, splashing to scare off the shark while the nurses rushed into the shallows to fetch the children.

Under the French regime, Malagasy prisoners (tax-evaders, cattle thieves, robbers, etc.) were retained to build roads, dig drainage ditches and perform other activities where manual labour was required. A group of them, working as stevedores and barge crew, heard the shouting, came dashing across the pier into the shallow water, grabbed the slow moving shark by its tail and hauled it up on the beach. Several of them having crowbars drove them into the shark, pinning and killing it.

It turned out to be a sand shark about ten feet long; it is a species which scrounges along the surf line catching small fish with its little needle-like teeth and is harmless to humans. The prisoners were delighted with their catch and promptly carved it up into small chunks to add to their regular prison fare of rice, manioc and vegetables. Once the shark was killed and the excitement had died down, things reverted to normal; the children playing in the shallows and their nannies watching them from the shore.

One Saturday, after a storm at sea, a group of us boys saw that glorious swells were hitting the beach beyond the protection of the harbour. The waves were breaking about thirty yards from the shore, their white-maned horses racing towards the shore and flinging themselves up the steep beach. Although we had never ventured outside the protection of the inner harbour before, the ideal swim-surfing conditions were irresistible. As we walked along the beach we saw four or five French school boys coming back towards the pier and the protection of the inner harbour. Saying, "Bon jour" in fractured French we let them know that we intended to do some swim surfing.

Looking alarmed they said, "Faites attention, il y a un requin là-bas." We smiled at them, shrugged our shoulders and walked on laughing among ourselves about those cautious cowardly 'Frogs.' "Why worry about a hurricane? If a hurricane comes we will have loads of time to get out of the water. The waves are wonderful!. Let's go!"

So we waded out waist deep, dove under the breakers letting the undertow take us beyond the breaking surf. Then, catching the bigger waves as they broke, we surfed back in on the cresting breakers into the shoaling waters, shooting fifteen or twenty feet up the beach to be stranded by the receding waves.

We were having a great time when suddenly someone yelled "Shark!" And there in a great wave was a shark, cutting in towards us. The shark, as sharks are wont to do, was swimming in, looking things over before carrying out an attack. Luckily everyone except me caught the crest of the wave and surfing like they were possessed, went swishing up the shoaling beach to safety.

I, being slightly farther out, missed the crest of the wave. The next thing that I knew I was on the back side of the breaker being sucked seaward by the backwash. There was nothing that I could do except wait and make certain that I caught the next wave just right if I was going to have any chance at all of getting to the beach before the 'hurricane' took a bite out of me.

Fortunately the next wave was a towering "one in seven," and I caught it just right. There I was, riding down a twelve foot wave, swimming for all I was worth. And there was the shark coming in on my right side to cut me off before I hit the beach. It was an appalling sight to those on the beach.

I was so terrified that my legs and arms were moving about as fast as the wings of a humming bird. Lucky for me, the shark hesitated just a bit too long, and both of us were swept into the shoaling water - he having to turn back and, never stopping swimming, I literally dug my way up the sandy beach as the wave receded.

Later on, when telling Cabi about what had happened, he exploded. "Hurricane! Requin! Vous êtes fous! Idiots!" And in much better English than we had French, he told us about a French boy who had been swim-surfing in Tamatave Harbour when a shark sliced off one of his arms. Instead of making for the beach the boy turned in the wave and tried to grab his lost arm out of the mouth of the shark. The shark then sliced off his second arm. He bled to death as he staggered out of the water.

* * * * *

The Great Garden

There was a great garden behind the two-roomed Missionary Children's School that covered about an acre of rich soil. Each student was allotted a small plot where they were obliged to plant a variety of vegetables to be watered, weeded, harvested and added to our diet in the Home. The garden also had good a variety of trees, the towering Coeur de Boeuf being so large that we spent hours playing "tree tag," climbing and jumping from one branch to another to avoid being be caught.

There was also a breadfruit tree which produced tough-skinned green fruit about the size of a volley ball. These were filled with a white pulp which held many soft, golden, sweet seeds. Breadfruit is one of the highest yielding food plants in the world. In 1787 Captain Bligh was in Tahiti busy loading the Bountry with hundreds of young shoots to be transplanted in the Caribbean to provide a bountiful source of food for the slaves, when the most famous mutiny in history took place and the plants were tossed into the sea.

There were also banana trees, orange, mandarin, lemon, papaya and avocado trees that made for great pickings. The sweet berries from the raspberry patch rarely made it to the dining room table as they were constantly being raided.

The outbreak of World War II and the fall of France led to Madagascar coming under the control of the Vichy Government rather than joining Charles De Gaulle and the Free French. This made us very aware of the precarious fortunes of war. I can still remember a verse of one of the songs we sang to the tune of Hark the Herald Angels Sing:

Sing the candle, sing the lamp,
Sing the concentration camp,
Sing of nations born anew,
Sing of exile for the Jew.
Praise the cunning submarine.
Wreath the world with evergreen.
Now the Christmas tide begets
Seven million bayonets.

So it was only to be expected that we started to dig a trench in the garden to emulate our betters and engage in trench warfare. After a while, discouraged by mud balls which simply did not have the quality of the snowballs we remembered so well and by the smarting pain caused by sling shots, we decided to dig a cave that angled out and downward from the trench.

Madagascar is famous for its rich red soil but because of the slash and burn method of cultivation leaving the land stripped of its forest covering, the soil erodes very easily during the rainy season. Hence Madagascar's age-old name, The Red Island. Astronauts looking down on Madagascar report that the silt pouring out from its rivers reddens the sea just as if the island is bleeding.

Digging in the garden soil was fairly easy as we never hit clay no matter how deep we delved into the red loam. So it did not take very long before we had an entrance shaft about foot and a half wide and two feet in height slanting away from the trench. After digging for about five feet, we started to carve out a cave that could readily hold four of us. Light was provided by candles and it was wonderful to sit there imagining that we were sappers digging under an enemy trench, packing it full of explosives and blowing them to smithereens.

Fortunately Mr. Anderson, who was staying in Fort Dauphin because of his wife's illness, decided to act as a quasi scout master. He soon found out what we doing and insisted that we collapse the roof of the cave before it collapsed on us. He agreed, however, that we could retain a cave-like sanctuary by laying two or three beams across the collapsed area if we covered them with some pieces of corrugated iron roofing and topped them off with a large pile of soil. The result was that, at one end of the trench we had what looked like a badly built machine gun nest. We were not happy campers!

So we diggers next got the bright idea to dig a vertical shaft straight down in the far corner of the dugout. Once we were down around four feet we dug a diagonal shaft. At its end, we carved out a larger cave than the one that had been destroyed. To prevent it from being discovered we covered the vertical shaft with a piece of flattened corrugated roofing; safe at last from the prying eyes of nosy adults!

If the first cave had collapsed on anyone, it is possible that he would have been able to push his way up through the red loam. If the lower cave had collapsed, no one inside would have been able to push his way through the red soil to safety. In short, if this second lower cave had collapsed, no one would have survived the weight of eight or nine feet of heavy red soil.

One Saturday morning, happy as clams and busy as beavers, Paul and Charles were enlarging the cave and filling pails with soil which the rest of us were hauling up and dumping, when Miss Thompson turned up to inspect our garden plots. Then, to our surprise, she walked over to take a look at what Mr. Anderson had disclosed to her.

We quickly covered the shaft with the piece of corrugated roofing and welcomed Miss Thompson with smiles. Encouraged by the warm reception she decided to climb down the short ladder into the open trench. Then to our alarm, she decided to enter into the covered portion of the trench, despite the warning that her clothes might get dirty. Thus Miss Thompson entered the Machine Gun Nest. Ignoring my plea, "Don't step there, Miss Thompson!" - she did.

The next thing she knew she was standing in the narrow shaft and hearing Paul's polite voice say, "Hello! Miss Thompson." Looking down, she saw a faint light coming from a small shaft by her feet. She didn't panic but calmly instructed us fetch the long ladder from the basement of the Home.

Once out of the shaft and the trench she did not go into hysterics. She merely said, in a voice that brooked no denial, that the second cave was to be collapsed, the trench and dugout was to be demolished, and the whole area was to revert to the its former state before we were infected by "wars and rumours of wars," as Scripture has it.

* * * * *

MIM

Catching Moray Eels

During our Long Vacation we used to walk out at low tide to the Lebanon Rock, on the leading edge of the long reef protecting the East Beach swimming area on the windward area of the peninsula leading to Lebanon. From there we could walk along the reef looking at all the different kinds of star fish, sea cucumbers, small fish and moray eels that lived in the small pools and sheltered sections of the reef. This of course led naturally to the urge to go fishing. No sooner said than done. So off we would go to purchase fishing line and hooks from Mong Chok, the Chinese merchant. We spent a great deal of time fishing during our long vacations.

It took a bit of patience, waiting for the fish to nibble on the bait, but it was a very pleasant pastime. Unfortunately the fish that we caught in the tidal pools were not very large so once they were caught we would usually toss them back into the pools to be eaten by those not stupid enough to have taken our bait. The moray eels would poke their heads out of holes in the coral. If you dangled a baited hook before their nose, they would take the bait but when you tried to set the hook, they would spit it out.

One pleasant morning at low tide, I was way out on the reef when I spotted a large moray poking its head out of a hole way down on the side of the reef. I decided to catch it without giving a thought to what I would do with it if I succeeded.

So, baiting my hook carefully, I dangled it just in front of the moray, which opened its mouth and swallowed it. Rather than setting the hook, I just let out more line and the moray kept on swallowing. After I figured the hook was about a foot into its gut, I gave sudden jerk, yanked the sucker right out of its hole. It landed right on the reef beside me.

Big mistake! The moray, over three feet long, was fighting mad and darted straight at me. I jumped back, still clutching the line, and naturally the moray just kept coming. I panicked, dropped the line and leaping to my left, I tripped and fell. I managed to avoid the moray but scraped a great deal of skin off my left knee. Losing the skin was painful enough but unfortunately I ended up with a great deal of shredded sharp coral particles embedded in my messy, open wound.

Getting up as quickly as possible, I picked my way ashore over the rough coral and took off for home and for help.

The washing of my knee and the picking out the broken bits of coral was very painful. Even more painful, however, was the iodine that my father insisted on painting over the whole area. Never again did I ever deliberately try to catch a moray. My next encounter with a much larger moray was not intentional but far more dramatic.

It happened early one Saturday morning when three or four of us were jigging for fish in Fort Dauphin between the end of the pier and the small landing at the bottom of the steep cliff below the main government building. There, the two main streets of the town met before becoming the single road leading to the Fort at the end of the headland that offered the very limited shelter of Fort Dauphin Bay. The only more sheltered area of the inner harbour was provided by the long, curved concrete pier and breakwater.

It was a very pleasant Saturday morning, the sun just having risen. We had already caught three or four small bottom feeders, when suddenly I had a very heavy tug on my line. "I've got a big one!" I yelled and started hauling in my line. The others quickly took in their lines so that my playing the fish would not foul their lines. Things couldn't have been better. We were finally getting a decent sized fish!

My catch broke the surface and I was so excited that, rather than taking a look at what I had on my line, I gave a great heave and flipped a great moray eel into the bottom of the boat. Of course we all leapt out of the boat into the water - the only solution as we were all bare-footed! Hanging onto the side of the boat we looked at the threshing monster and wondered what we should do.

Cubby solved the problem by handing me a clasp knife and ordered me to get back into the boat and kill it. I carefully worked my way over the prow of the boat, and, reaching down among the floor boards took a swipe at the moray. All it did was to make it even angrier. But Cubby was even more angry, so I kept slashing away, slowly hacking off sections which merely kept on twisting and turning on their own. Eventually, however, I managed to cut it into enough pieces to kill it.

That being done the others climbed back into the boat and I took a great deal of pepper as we paddled back to the beach. The most cruel cut of all was when they suggested that I take the chunks of moray home for supper.

* * * * *

MİM

Crocodiles

As children we were always fascinated by crocodiles, stories of crocodiles and the possibility of hunting crocodiles. After all, they were the only animals in Madagascar that comprised a major threat to humans. They lurked in rivers, marshes and lagoons and the Malagasy, especially the unwary women who did their washing in the rivers, were often attached by crocodiles. They would seize their unsuspecting victims,* drown them by rolling them over and over in the water and then conceal the bodies in deep undercuts in river banks only to be eaten after they had sufficiently decayed to make a tasty morsel. In Ranomafana a large crocodile was once shot by the local French administrator and slit open; inside the stomach were found decorative silver bracelets that the locals were able to identify as belonging to several women who had been lost over the years; they had disappeared when doing their washing on the river bank.

Crocodile teeth are not solid like those of a lion or tiger nor do they have molars; they are peg-shaped and many layered teeth that stack like ice cream cones or paper cups. Thus, if the tooth is older and there is enough resistance in biting, it breaks and remains in the flesh of the victim. The crocodile lets go and grows another tooth.

Thus it happened that a woman who had managed to break free from a crocodile attack came rushing up to the hill to the Station to see what my Father could do, as crocodile bites are naturally very infectious. As Father always had a small wooden jar of raw opium in his medical kit, (it was dark brown and had the constituency of heavy honey) he gave her enough opium to kill the pain. He then squeezed open the wounds, extracted any teeth he found and cleaned out the punctured wounds with iodine or whatever other powerful disinfectant was available.

In those days there was not a stigma attached to opium in Madagascar and Father often used it to sedate natives who had broken or dislocated limbs before trying to re-set them. Only rarely would there be a medical doctor available in Ranomafana. There were lady missionaries who, such as Sister Anna, were deaconesses trained as registered nurses and who were stationed in Fort Dauphin. Sister Anna used to travel to the various mission stations if someone was seriously ill.

A common pastime on our Short Vacation was for Erling and I to man the ferry at the crossing of the river between the east side of the Ambolo Valley and the village of Ranomafana. The ferry consisted of two large Malagasy dugouts hacked out from large trees and connected by three beams supporting a wooden platform that was about ten feet long and eight feet wide. It could easily support a loaded ox-cart or eight or ten people along with the produce they were taking to market such as sacks of rice, other heavy items or produce.

There was a long wire cable, spanning the river at about ten feet above the water, that supported a plank which slid along the cable by means of grooved wheels attached at each end. The ferry was connected to the sliding plank by ropes attached at each end. All we had to do to make the ferry cross the river was to shorten the rope at the end of the ferry facing the bank of the river where we wanted to go and lengthen the rope at the end of the ferry opposite the bank that we wanted to leave. The current pushing against the angled ferry then caused it to move across the river. Once we reached the other side and the passengers had unloaded and re-loaded, we simply reversed the length of the rope at each end and returned to the side of the river that we had just left.

We were fascinated by being able to cross a wide river without anyone having to paddle and spent many happy hours running the ferry. The Tanosy, who appreciated the pleasure of resting** must have been highly amused at being ferried across the river by slightly demented Vazaha (white) boys playing at being ferrymen.

Father had been raised by pioneering parents first in the Dakota Territories and later near Donalda, Alberta. Mother's parents (Lefsruds) had settled first in Montana, then near Gruouard, in northern Alberta even before the province had established the survey lines. There, grandma's oldest sons attended the Catholic mission along with the local Indians, thus learning Cree on the playground and reading in school. The Lefsruds would still be there if Karin had not convinced her land-speculating husband that she had not left Norway just to raise her boys as Indians! They finally homesteaded on excellent land about twelve miles north of Viking.

With such backgrounds neither of our parents seemed to have any qualms about letting us "go out and play" as long as we turned up at meal times. Neither of them were infected with the modern nonsense about protecting children from all possible harm even to the extent of taking slides and swings out of playgrounds because even under adult supervision some little child might possibly be hurt to howls of outrage from parent and chortles of delight from *injury lawyers.*

We also used to go down to where the river ran right against the foot of the hill and wade in the shallows along the bank. It was there that we found a vein of very pure clay which we used to mould small animals, pots and dishes, etc. and leave them in hot sun to dry and would pick them up the next day.

One of my most vivid memories was the morning when we were playing out on a little sand bar where we had waded, carrying some clay from the river bank. We were busy amusing ourselves with the clay when suddenly I noticed that there were little triangle-shaped pieces of wood slowly floating upstream in the shallows between us and the shore. The piece furthest up stream was about the size of a small fist, followed by two smaller pieces of wood about a foot behind the leader and separated from each other by about eight inches or so. I watched it for a while, surprised at three pieces of wood working themselves up stream against the current.

"Look at that!" I said, "I wonder if it is a crocodile?" I threw a good sized stone and struck it right between what turned out to be the nose and the eyes. A small crocodile, more surprised than I, flipped itself in the air and turned down-stream. I cannot recall if we told our parents about the incident but as children we were very aware that the less our parents knew about what we were doing, all the better. So, I don't think that we did.

That was my first encounter with crocodiles. My second encounter took place the year before we left Madagascar but that is another story to be entitled "My First Crocodile and How I Didn't Shoot It."

* *The crocodile seizes and the water suffocates* Tanosy Proverb.

** Father once took a picture of a man hired to do ladder work cleaning the windows of the church whom he found fast asleep on the ladder.

* * * * *

Getting ready for a day looking for crocodiles

Erling   Leif

Removing a Tribal Curse

The lives of the Malagasy are not only strictly regulated by long established customs but in addition, certain actions that are held to be so heinous that committing one would bring a curse not only upon the transgressor but, in some cases, upon the family or even the tribe. Such taboos or 'fady' are so binding that even the highly educated or 'Europeanise' Malagasy will not readily violate age-old prohibitions any more than an orthodox Jew will roast pork in his kitchen. Different tribes had different 'fady.' *What was sauce for the goose was not sauce for the gander*, to mangle an old English maxim.

Now, one of the ways that the French got the roads, dams, drainage ditches and other public works that required a great deal of manual labour, was to levy the corvée on all healthy Malagasy. This levy had roots in the feudal system when peasants were tied to the land and forced to work for a set number of days for the local lord or squire. It was highly resented and was one of the first injustices abolished by the French Revolution. Malagasy could avoid the corvée by paying an equivalent tax but the great majority of the tribal people had to work off their corvée.

Now it happened that a small group of Tandroy, the tribe that lived west of the mountains on the dry interior plains, had been sent to the Ambolo Valley to fulfil their annual corvée obligation. This was very troublesome to them as the Tandroy and Tanosy were not only age-old tribal enemies but also had different customs and taboos.

For well over three hundred years Madagascar was the centre of a very profitable slave trade as the tribes had no qualms at all about selling each other to Arab and European slave traders who cruised the coastal waters and who often had fortified trading posts where slaves gathered. Since the Malagasy counted their personal wealth in cattle, nothing could have been more pleasing to Tandroy raiders than coming home to their dry plains with captives and a lowing herd of fat Tanosy cattle. Once the French annexed the Island in 1896, they put an end to all inter-tribal raids and warfare, but just like the rest of humanity, old animosities died slowly.

So Father was not too surprised when one morning, six large muscular Tandroy turned up outside his study. He was surprised however, when after very cordial greetings, he was asked to listen to their tale of woe. It seemed that they did not object so much to the corvée but on the whole their lives in the Valley were not going that well. Not only did the Tanosy have many foolish customs but what was 'fady' to the Tandroy was quite acceptable to Tanosy.

For example, the Tanosy had no qualms at all about eating turtle, something totally taboo to any self-respecting Tandory. Of course, as Father pointed out, that should be no great hardship. While the dry plains of Androy were noted for their abundance of large tortoise, the Valley did not have many turtles. Obviously that was not the real problem, as they readily agreed. They were, however, really between a *rock and a hard place* when everyone else at a party was having a good time eating and drinking but the pièce de résistance was roast boar. Surely, a man as widely travelled as he, knew that eating wild boar or domestic pig was 'fady' - an absolute anathema to pious Tandroy. Surely a religious man such as himself knew that their ancestors would do more than turn in their graves if any of them committed such a sacrilege.

"Ah!" said Father, leaning back in his chair, and staring at the ceiling. "I can see that you have a very serious problem; something that needs a great deal of study. Please make yourselves comfortable while I look more deeply into this matter." *

He sighed and looked at the many books on his shelves for a long time. Then he got up, took down the third volume of *Commentaries on Luther's Catechism*, paged through it carefully and made a few notes. He then opened his massive *Dramatic Works of William Shakespeare*, frowned deeply and penned a few more notes. He next referred to the fourth volume of 'The Encyclopaedia Britannica,' looked a bit perplexed, and finally he consulted colourful pages of the large 'World Atlas.' **

Pondering his notes thoughtfully he broke into a smile and said, "Friends, I think I have found the remedy. Please wait here patiently while I go and make up a powerful potion that should remove any 'fady' that might harm you. I will soon be back." He left the office, went into the small room where the medical supplies for the mission were stored, mixed up large container with warm water, Epsom Salts, a castor oil emetic and anything else that would totally flush out the alimentary canal.

Returning to his study he stirred the container rapidly with a large ladle, filled a very large glass with the mixture and said. "Friends, I believe that this will rid your bodies of any Fady you may have. All of you must, in turn, drink a large glass of this potent mixture. You must swallow it without any stopping so as not to break the charm. When all of you have finished the drinking I will give you further instructions."

When they had all finished drinking the mixture he then said. "All of you did very well. Now you are going to walk slowly to the bottom of the hill on the down wind side. Do not go back to town but remain there quietly there until the spirits move you. Once this powerful medicine has taken its course you may feel a bit feeble. Do not worry, you will be freed from all 'fady' and will be able to eat or drink whatever you like."

A week of so later they turned up all smiles. "The strong medicine you gave us worked in a most powerful manner. We now have no 'fady' problems at all living among the Tanosy."

* Father was very interested in the beliefs and customs of the Malagasy and received from the University of Minnesota his M.A in Anthropology for his thesis on their beliefs and customs. He would never insult them by being dismissive or scornful. Obviously he is not the first 'doctor' who cured a malady with a placebo. If he had not listened sympathetically or if he had told them that their beliefs were nonsense, they would have left the Mission convinced that he was a witless, arrogant Vazaha who, despite his preaching about a loving God, really didn't care for them at all.

** Of course when Father told me of this event he did not detail all the conversation. I remember his extensive library. We still have the massive 'Dramatic Works of William Shakespeare' which he brought back to Canada at the end of his last term in 1963.

* * * * *

Leif steering the boat sailing in Madagascar

Messing around in Boats

Although I hated having my face, hair, ears and hands washed when I was a kid, I was always fascinated by water in quantities larger than a wash basin or tub could hold. Puddles, ponds, streams, rivers, lakes and seas have had a bewitching attraction that I have never been able to resist. One of my earliest memories of water is of our family going in a car to a lake, of a picnic being laid out on beach and of us being so utterly fascinated by the glittering waves dancing in the sunlight. I was so fascinated that I walked right out into the water, not stopping at all until the waves were splashing my face. I once asked Mother of this strange memory and she told me it actually happened.

Apparently they had gone for a picnic on the banks of Dried Meat Lake, situated south east of Camrose. While they got things laid out for lunch I stood still - a miracle in itself - and then set out walking straight into the water until it was right up to my head. I must have more than a healthy dose of Viking genes somewhere in my make-up.

The East Beach lay between Fort Dauphin and the missionary summer cottages at Lebanon. It was protected by a long reef about three hundred feet off shore. The reef ran from the Lebanon Rock about a quarter of a mile back to Fort Dauphin. Although the beach was not as sheltered from the wind as West Beach, if the waves were breaking over the reef there was a considerable undertow. It was there that Mission's Bath House had been built because there was no chance that sharks or manta rays would venture inside the reef.

We became very familiar with the East Beach as, during the school year when the weather was good, our teachers would take us there for our after school or Saturday swimming. During the Long Vacations we used to walk out to the Lebanon Rock and pick our way along the outer reef during low tide. We would take a poke at the creatures in the crevasses or dangle our lines to catch the many small fish. On a warm afternoon, one of the missionaries would reluctantly agree to take thirty kids down to East Beach for a cool dip.

The boys and girls changing rooms were separated by ship-lap boards, had hooks on the walls and benches on the side opposite the door. Ever curious, we boys had cut away the overlapping section of the ship-lap on their side at a few strategic spots so we could peek at the girls while we and they were changing. Of course being caught peeking was shameful; not being caught was praiseworthy, at least among the boys.

One afternoon, when dressing after a swim, I decided to "take a look" only to find a blue eye already staring through the hole from the girl's side. Louise, the love of my life, quicker on the draw than I, shouted "Leif, you're peeking!" Miss Rorstad, lacking even the most rudimentary power of analysis, dismissed my reasoned argument that if Louise saw me peeking, she must have been peeking first. I was a fool to think that Miss Rorstad had any interest in justice. Since she had been changing with the girls, she must have realized that I, her most detested student, may have enjoyed a careful examination of her in the nude, thus destroying her limited sense of justice.

Over the years she always had a smile of self-satisfaction when giving me 'Red Fs' on my report card for Conduct/Behaviour. It could be traced to the time when the second hand of her wrist watch began vibrating back and forward. This mystery was solved when a rat squealed on me and told her I had run a strong horseshoe magnet over her watch which she used to leave on her desk while teaching. Oddly enough, at about that same time, Miss Rorstad had become remarkably biased against me. As a teacher she must have known that her brilliant lesson on magnetism was bound to inspire me to further individual research.

This whole incident has caused me to instinctively take the male side over the female side in disputes. It may also explain why I have found John Knox's pamphlet, "*The First Blast of the Trumpet Against the Monstrous Regimen of Women*" so theologically profound.

* * * * *

About the author

Leif was born on June 14, 1929, son of Peter and Ragna Stolee, serving a first term as Lutheran missionaries in Southern Madagascar. His father had trained as a fighter pilot during the First World War but Germany surrendered before he was sent overseas. After he had received a Bachelor of Education degree from the University of Alberta, Peter volunteered to go to Madagascar as a high school principal. Having spent a year at the Sorbonne in Paris to qualify to teach in the French Colonial system, he was appointed the director of the equivalent of a junior college training Malagasy for employment in business, colonial administration, or as catechists to help in the spreading of the gospel.

After completing their first seven year term the Stolees returned to Canada. Due to the great depression of 1929, the Lutheran Church did not have enough money to send the Stolees back to Madagascar, so after he was ordained as Pastor in St. Paul, Minnesota and his furlough overseas was accepted, Peter served as a pastor at Lea Park, Alberta until the family was sent again to Madagascar in 1936. This time he was assigned to the mission at Ranamafana "Hot Springs" that was famous for its lemurs. Meanwhile, his children, Elinor, Erling, Leif and James, were placed in the Missionary Children's Boarding school at Fort Dauphin. There Leif completed his elementary education.

In 1945 after the Second World War, the Stolees returned to Canada where Leif completed high school at Camrose Lutheran College. Since a missionary's salary was not that great, Leif worked on his uncle's farm during the summer and on the threshing crew in the fall. In his last two years in high school, he and his brother Erling both worked in the saw mills and in the forests of British Columbia cutting timber.

At this time the Korean War was going full blast, so Erling and Leif financed their education by enrolling in the University Naval Training Division as cadets. They trained at HMCS Nonsuch naval base in Edmonton during the winter and spent the summer months training at Esquimalt and on frigates in order to qualify as Sub Lieutenants.

After completing his Bachelor of Arts in history and philosophy, Leif obtained the rank of Lieutenant in the Royal Canadian Naval Reserve. Over the years, he served as a watch keeping officer on a research vessel on the West Coast inlets and the Great Lakes, training sea cadets during the summer. He served on the HMCS Oriole, the ninety foot ketch that sailed from Halifax to Bermuda and then via the Panama Canal up the west coast of Esquimalt, where it was employed at Royal Roads anchorage in training cadets to be officers. Leif spent nearly a year serving in a minesweeping squadron patrolling up and down the West Coast.

He then became a qualified diver, first training on the old fashioned diving gear. Leif then became a frogman and a demolition diver whose purpose was to defuse mines dropped by enemies in harbours. He decided to resign and get his Bachelor of Education Degree. On his return to Edmonton, he heard that the Lieutenant Commander in charge of Diving and Demolitions had been killed. He had been attempting to defuse a Japanese mine whose mooring line rusted so that it drifted across the Pacific, landing on a beach on the West Coast.

Leif then joined his brother James and two others to visit almost every country in Europe in a Volkswagen bus, as pre-hippie hippies. On his return to London, broke, Leif started his teaching career. After nearly a year, he resigned to make a tour of Ireland and return to Edmonton, where he began teaching at Eastwood Junior High.

Leif and his first wife, Greta, who had had cancer, adopted three children, Peter, Erling, and Rachel. After ten years, he transferred to Harry Ainlay High. He was very active in the Alberta Teacher's Association and became the District Representative for Edmonton Local. In 1969, he took a sabbatical and received his Master of Arts Degree, in history and philosophy. Becoming too critical about the actions of the ATA executive he eventually lost his position, much to the satisfaction of the Executive Council and the docile, sheep-like general membership.

He was an outspoken critic of what he saw to be a shift from teacher-centred to student-centered education and a decline in the academic standards in Alberta schools. With actions speaking louder than words:-

- in 1991 Leif co-founded Albertans for Quality Education.
- In 1994, he started the Southwest Edmonton Charter School Association.
- in 1995, he played a vital role in launching the Cogito Alternative Program of teacher-based instruction.

The Cogito program was designed to achieve academic excellence, through the acquisition of knowledge and skills, and the ability to think critically and independently. Old Scona Academic High School became a showcase for Cogito under Leif as the founding principal.

In 1977, Peter Lougheed, impressed by Leif's independence, arranged for him to receive from the Governor General *Her Majesty the Queen's Twenty Fifth Anniversary Medal* for his contribution to education in Alberta. Sometime later Leif also received the *Distinguished Alumnus Award for Outstanding Achievement in His Field* from Camrose Lutheran College.

Leif was appointed Social Studies Coordinator for Edmonton Public, a position he held until, fed up with the bureaucracy, he returned to Harry Ainlay as Vice Principal. He held that position until he retired to take care of his wife, Greta who was dying from cancer.

After the death of his wife, Leif left the Lutheran Church and became a Roman Catholic. He met and married Liz McNab, becoming a stepfather to Mark and Dmitri, the latter adopting Leif by changing his surname to Stolee.

A parish priest, on a two year assignment from India, asked Leif for a donation to help a small orphan home. Rather than giving him $1000 Leif decided to set up an organization to provide continued support and growth. On December 17, 2005 the society for the education and assistance of rural Indian children (SEARIC) was formed with the help of local Canadians together with Sikhs and Hindus, who had come from India. Being an accredited Canadian entity with legal status in India, Leif's charitable organisation has been amazingly successful. It has raised more the $300,000, a return of over 300 times on the original $1000.

* * * * *

Manufactured by Amazon.ca
Bolton, ON